Contents

Directions in the cul-de-sac	5	Directions in	9
Directions in the school area	6	Wood Island	20
Directions to school	7	Distances near school	21
Make a compass tracing	8	Flying frim Birmingham	22
Directions in school	9	Flying from Zurich	23
Simple compass directions	10	Distances in the western USA	24
More compass directions	11	Distances in the eastern USA	25
Signpost map	12	Distances around	26–27
Signpost map at the show	13	Direct distance, actual distance	28
Signpost map of Linton	14–15	More direct distances, actual distances	29
Directions from Britain	16	Whitby – air view and map	30–31
Directions in Europe	17	Planning a classroom	32

Teachers' notes

The aim of the activities in this book is to support the implementation of the National Curriculum for Geography, with particular reference to Attainment Target 1 – Geographical skills. These activities should not be seen as teaching tools in themselves, but as opportunities for children to practise newly-acquired skills. To maximise their benefit, it is important at the outset to explain carefully the purpose of each one to the children. In this way they can focus on the key aspects of the activity and derive maximum benefit. It would also be useful to have large-scale (1:2,500 or 1:1,250 or 1:1,000) Ordnance Survey maps of the local area, as well as the 1:25,000 and 1:50,000 sheets, available for use and displayed around the classroom throughout the activities. In this way, children will become familiar with seeing and using Ordnance Survey maps and will perceive them as a useful tool rather than an intimidating document of the local area. Similarly, a set of up-to-date atlases should be available which the children can consult when attempting some of the later activities in the book.

The aims of this book

The aims of this book are:
• to introduce children to basic ideas of direction, specifically the four and eight points of the compass and of distance;
• to extend the children's understanding of the role of distance and direction on maps;
• to provide practice for the development of mapping skills;
• to enable children to build on earlier map skills in order to develop increased competencies;
• to provide mapwork activities which are fun and enjoyable yet challenging to a wide range of abilities.

Geographical content

The development of skills in understanding, interpreting and using maps is fundamental in geography. These are the skills upon which other geographical work will be based. Hence it is important for children to be able to use maps fluently and confidently. Generally, the development of mapwork skills is best achieved within the context of other studies. Thus, for example, a study of the local area will be based on examination of a range of maps of that area. Similarly, any study of distant places needs to be placed in context by the use of atlases, globes and maps.

This book provides activities and opportunities to develop mapwork skills in relation to the specific ideas of distance and direction. The aim is to make mapwork fun and an enjoyable exercise for the children. Hence the activities are often presented as challenges or games based on aspects of everyday life or even adventure stories. In this way, by practising these activities, children will be able to develop their understanding of grids and symbols on a range of different types of maps. Such activities are an important preliminary to the study of the full range of Ordnance Survey maps. Children find Ordnance Survey maps of whatever scale, from 1:1,250 to 1:50,000, difficult documents to understand. The teacher's role is to break down this seemingly complex document into a series of readily understandable parts. In this way teachers will be able to provide children with the key to the 'mysteries' of Ordnance Survey maps. Thus children can work on understanding distance and direction before they see a full Ordnance Survey map. Similarly, they can work on aspects of maps such as distance and direction or plan views before they begin to see how the various parts of the map eventually combine to make the whole picture.

It is therefore important to organise children's work in developing map skills so that all achieve success in their activities. In this way, as with other aspects of their learning, they will come to see maps as useful tools in the understanding of the geography of an area. They will also become increasingly familiar with the vast detail contained within a map and become increasingly proficient in interpreting and using that data. Children's natural curiosity becomes engaged rapidly once they understand what a map does and does not show. Their interest and eagerness to use maps is related directly to the teacher's own map interest and ability. Hence it is particularly important that teachers develop their own skills and confidence in mapwork, which can then be passed on to their pupils. It is hoped that the activities in this book may prove to be as valuable to the teacher as to the children.

Notes on individual activities

Pages 5, 6 and 7: Directions in the cul-de-sac, Directions in the school area and Directions to school

Aim: to revise some of the earlier work children may have attempted in relation to describing direction in terms of either 'opposite', 'next to', 'beyond' or four cardinal points of the compass. These activities will give the teacher a good diagnostic guide to the level of understanding of individual children, so that some may need further revision of basic principles and others may be able to progress more rapidly through the material.
Extension: Ask the children to draw some simple maps of their own route to school or of the school site, and give directions either in terms of 'opposite', 'next to' and so on, or north, south, east and west.

Pages 8, 9, 10 and 11: Make a compass tracing, Directions in school, Simple compass directions and More compass directions

Aim: to familiarise children with the eight points of the compass. The compass tracing is easy to make and is a constant reminder of the terminology used in compass directions. It can be used in the teacher's own school but a real compass should be used first to find all the main points and perhaps the walls of the classroom labelled N, S, E, W. Then the children can give directions within the school or classroom having correctly orientated their own tracing. All the examples on pages 9, 10 and 11 use the idea of north being at the top of the map. Make sure that the children adjust the lines on their tracing when placing them over the cross on the maps to ensure that north-south is vertical and east-west is horizontal.
Extension: ask the children to draw their own squares, similar to those on pages 10 and 11, add their own symbols then set questions for a partner on directions within their square. The partners should then attempt the questions. For some children the teacher may want to change the postion of north so that it lies to one side of the page, then ask them to give new directions for the features.

Pages 12, 13, 14 and 15: Signpost map, Signpost map at the show and Signpost map of Linton (1 and 2)

Aim: to encourage children to use the simple device of the signpost map as a way of becoming confident in giving directions using the eight points of the compass. Page 12 is a simple introduction to using the signpost map and children can draw their own locations in the class in relation to other pupils. Page 13 uses a different context to develop the same ideas of the eight points of the compass. The Signpost map of Linton on pages 14 and 15 shows how the idea can be developed for use on maps and plans. Children who rush through the activities on pages 12 and 13 may find pages 14 and 15 harder going. In all cases north has been retained at the top of the map.
Extension: Change the direction of north on the map on page 14 to the left- or right-hand side of the page. Now ask the children to redraw some of the signpost maps with the new north point.

Pages 16, 17, 18 and 19: Directions from Britain, Directions in Europe, Directions in the USA (1 and 2)

Aim: to encourage children to use the skills and knowledge they have acquired on direction in the context of maps. For Directions from Britain the children will need an up-to-date atlas and it may be useful for some children to place their compass tracing over the UK to help name the countries in different directions. Page 17 uses a map of Europe for the questions but teachers may want to use different atlas maps of Europe to extend the activity. Directions in the USA uses an area with which most pupils are not readily familiar and can be used as an assessment activity to identify individual degrees of progress in using directions correctly.
Extension: tell the children to set different questions for each other using the maps on pages 17 and 18.

Pages 20 and 21: Wood Island and Distances near school

Aim: to revise simple ideas about measuring distances on maps and using the scale on maps. Wood Island retains the use of measuring straight-line distances in centimetres, but Distances near school moves on to the way in which such distances can be translated into actual distances on the ground. Some children may need more practice at making this transition.

Extension: Ask the children to draw their own maps of a real or imaginary area like the one on page 21, then tell them to measure distances and set questions for each other.

Pages 22, 23, 24 and 25: Flying from Birmingham, Flying from Zurich, Distances in western USA, Distances in eastern USA

Aim: to give children practice in measuring straight-line distances between towns and using a scale to convert this measurement into kilometres. On pages 22 and 23 tell the children to use a ruler to connect Birmingham and Zurich to every other city on the map. Stress that all the lines must start from Birmingham or Zurich. On pages 24 and 25 straight-line distances are again employed, but taken a stage further with the tours described. Here pupils have to measure distances along a route to find the total number of kilometres covered.

Extension: ask the children to devise their own tours of the UK, Europe and the USA (West and East), and work out the total distances for their tours, then get other children to measure the routes and compare totals.

Pages 26 and 27: Distances around

Aim: to show the children that not all distances are in a straight line. Often we may talk about places being 'within a radius of...' The children should use a pair of compasses to draw the circles shown on page 26. Tell them not to worry if not all the circumferences of the larger circles fit on their A4 sheet. Then tell them to align the cross on page 26 with that on the map on page 27 before attempting to answer the questions.

Extension: ask the children to mark other features on the map such as more bus stops or post boxes or street lights or litter bins, and then get them to give the distance from the centre of the school.

Pages 28 and 29: Direct distance, actual distance and More direct distance, actual distance

Aim: to show children how to measure non straight-line distances on a map. Some children may need quite a lot of practice in laying a piece of string or wool along a route which bends to follow roads and so on, and then reading off the total distance from the scale. However, it is important to stress that usually, direct distances (as the crow flies) are shorter than actual distances.

Extension: Make up other journeys on the two maps and ask the children to compare straight-line distances with actual distances. Ask the children to draw their own maps and devise tasks to measure direct and actual distances.

Pages 30 and 31: Whitby air view and map (1 and 2)

Aim: to remind children of the reality of the landscape and how this is shown on a map where distance and direction can be given. The drawing shows an oblique aerial view of Whitby looking north. It is the equivalent of an aerial photograph. Make sure the children can identify the same features on both the drawing and the map before they attempt to give directions and measure distances.

Extension: Mark other features on the map of Whitby and ask the children to measure direct and actual distances between them.

Page 32: Planning a classroom

Aim: to show how measurements on a map can be used for a practical purpose with regard to designing the layout of a classroom. Ensure that the children understand the scale of the map of the classroom and the features which are already marked. Tell them to cut out copies of the shapes for tables (two sizes), chairs, and storage units. Now ask them to think about the best arrangement of tables, units and chairs within the classroom space.

Extension: Encourage each child to suggest two alternative layouts and then say why one is better than the other.

National Curriculum: Geography

The activities in this book support the following requirements of the PoS for KS2 from the geography National Curriculum:

Geographical Skills
Pupils should be taught to develop and apply the following geographical skills:
- to identify and describe geographical features and conditions, using simple instruments, *eg rain gauges, clinometers, compasses*, to make measurements;
- select and use relevant information from a variety of sources;
- measuring and recording accurately;
- interpreting information from maps and plans by developing a range of map skills (using coordinates and four-figure grid references, using symbols and keys, measuring direction and distance, following routes);
- using maps and photographs, including oblique aerial photographs, to identify features and relationships;
- making and using their own maps and plans at a variety of scales.

Places
Pupils should be taught:
- to locate, using globes, maps or atlases, places that they are studying.

Scottish 5-14 Curriculum: Environmental studies – Social subjects

Attainment outcome	Strand	Attainment targets	Level
Understanding people and place	Knowledge and understanding	Making and using maps: • using left and right and reference to landmarks in given directions; • using scale and relative location to interpret information on maps.	C
	Collecting evidence	Extract specific information from maps.	C
	Recording and presenting	Complete simple tables.	C

Northern Ireland Curriculum: Geography

Attainment Target 1: Methods of Geographical Enquiry
Pupils should have opportunities to:
- explore plans/maps at different scales;
- measure straight line and curved distances between two points using the linear scale printed on the map;
- use the eight points of the compass;
- recognise the need for symbols on Ordnance Survey maps;
- locate places in atlases using the contents page, the index, and latitude and longitude;
- use aerial photographs for example, *oblique photographs*.

Attainment Target 4: Place and Space
Pupils should have opportunities to become familiar with:
- the countries and major cities of Europe.

● Name _____

Directions in the cul-de-sac

Below is a map of a cul-de-sac. It is a road that is a dead end. The map also has a compass which shows directions.
● Use the compass to answer the following questions.
• In what direction are you looking if you look:
   (a) down the road from the supermarket?
   (b) towards the houses from the bank?
   (c) towards the post office from the houses?
   (d) towards the supermarket as you walk down the road?
• Which building stretches from east to west?
• Which is further south, the bank or the post office?
• Give compass directions to describe the postman's walk as he goes from A, then delivers to all the houses and then goes to B.

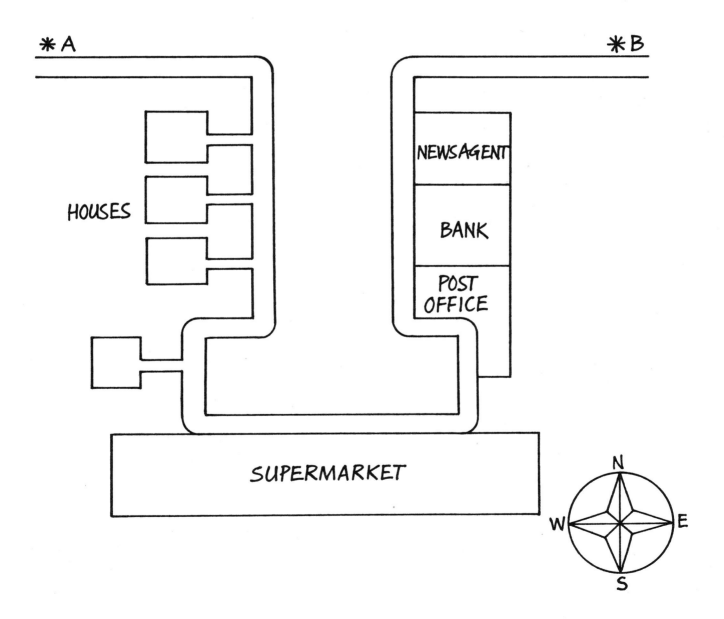

ESSENTIALS FOR GEOGRAPHY: Distance and direction

● Name _____

Directions in the school area

● Look at the map of the area around Grantley School. Now answer the following questions:
- Which building is **opposite** the grocers?
- What shop is **next** to the chemist?
- Which building is **left of** the vet's surgery?
- Which building is **behind** the Doctor's surgery?
- Which building is **opposite** the sports centre?
- Which shop is **right of** the Post Office?
- Which building is **opposite** the fire station?
- What is **in front of** the Post Office?

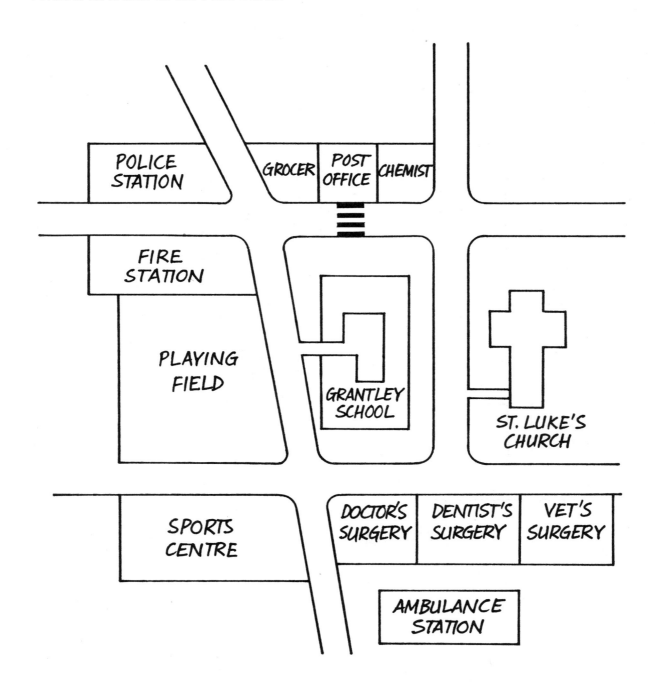

● ESSENTIALS FOR GEOGRAPHY: Distance and direction

- Name _____

Directions to school

The picture map below shows Mark's journey to school.
- Look at the map and finish the description of his journey to school by writing where he turns right or left.

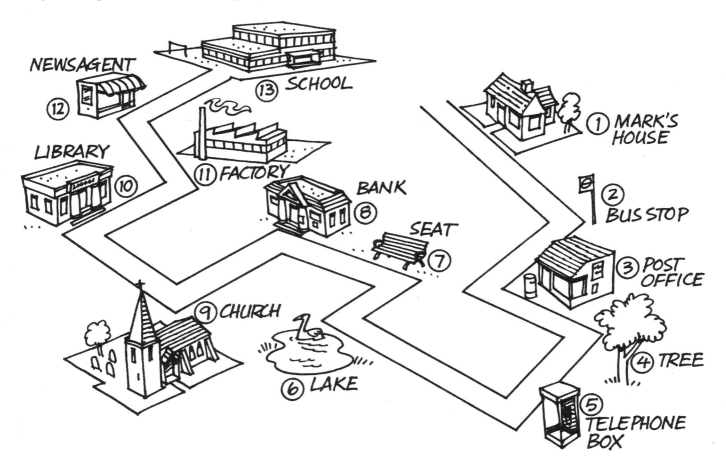

Mark's journey to school

1. Mark leaves home.
2. He turns right at the bus stop.
3. He turns _____ at the _____ .
4. He turns _____ at the _____ .
5. He turns _____ at the _____ .
6. He turns _____ at the _____ .
7. He turns _____ at the _____ .
8. He turns _____ at the _____ .
9. He turns _____ at the _____ .
10. He turns _____ at the _____ .
11. He turns _____ at the _____ .
12. He turns _____ at the _____ .
13. He arrives at school.

ESSENTIALS FOR GEOGRAPHY: Distance and direction

● Name _____

Make a compass tracing

● Use a sheet of tracing paper and carefully trace the compass shape below:

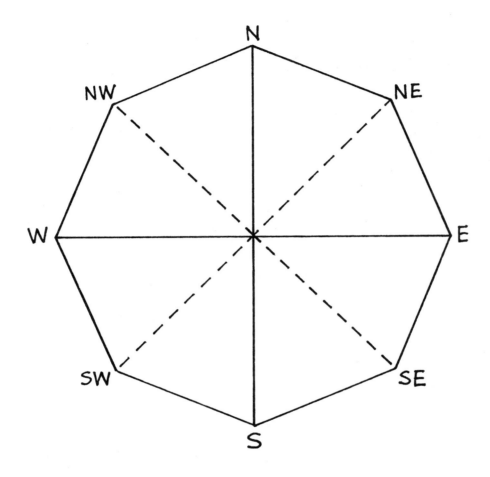

● Print on the main directions, N. for north, N.W. for north-west and so on.
● Make sure all the heavy north-south and east-west lines, plus the broken lines cross exactly in the centre.

The tracing can now be used on maps and plans to find answers to questions about direction. Remember that when you use the tracing the north-south line must be absolutely vertical and the east-west line must be absolutely horizontal.

● ESSENTIALS FOR GEOGRAPHY: Distance and direction

Directions in school

You will need the compass tracing from page 8.
● Place the tracing on the map of the school, so that it its centre lies exactly in the middle of the cross shown between classrooms 4 and 6.
● Make sure that the north-south line of the tracing is vertical and that the east-west line is horizontal.

Now answer the following questions by giving a direction (N, S, E, W, NE, NW, SW, SE):
- On which side of the school is the office?
- On which side of the school is the hall?
- On which side of the school are toilets 1?
- On which side of the school are toilets 2?

Slide the tracing paper (keeping it upright) over the centre of the gym. You can see that the staff room lies to the NE (north-east). Now fill in these gaps:
- The hall lies _____ of the gym.
- The store lies _____ of the gym.
- Classroom 4 lies _____ of the gym.
- The head teacher's room lies _____ of the gym.

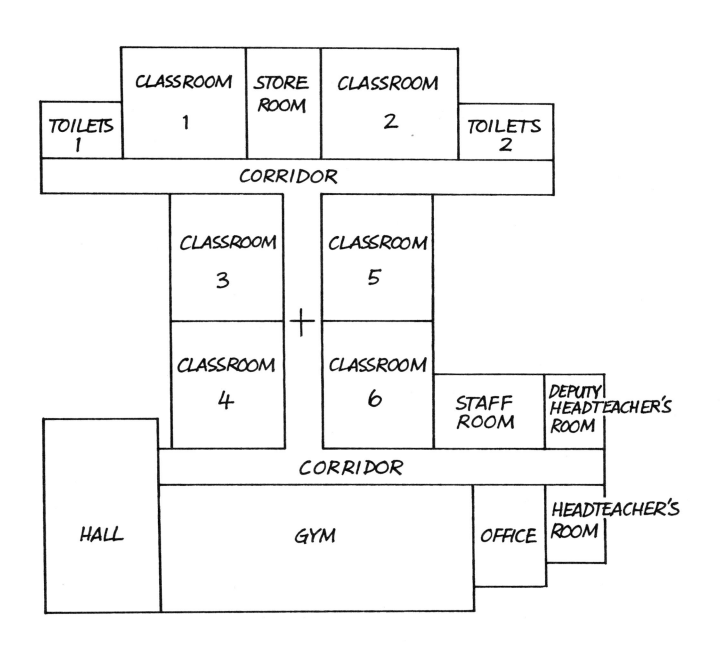

ESSENTIALS FOR GEOGRAPHY: Distance and direction

Simple compass directions

● Put the compass tracing from page 8 over the two lines in the centre of the picture below. Make sure the north-south line is vertical and the east-west line horizontal.

● Now use compass tracing to answer the following questions:
- What is south of Julie?_____
- What is north of Julie?_____
- What is west of Julie?_____

● Fill in the gaps with the correct direction:
- The school is _____ on the map.
- The church is _____ on the map.
- The pub is _____ on the map.
- The trees are _____ on the map.

● Now fill in these gaps:
- The trees are _____ of the office block.
- The lake is _____ of the school.
- The factory is _____ of the lake.
- The school is _____ of the office block.
- The pub is _____ of the office block.
- The church is _____ of the lake.

● Give the direction you would go in if you went:
- from the trees to Julie _____
- from the factory to the school _____
- from the lake to the office block _____
- from the school to the church _____

● ESSENTIALS FOR GEOGRAPHY: Distance and direction

● Name _____

More compass directions

● Put the compass tracing from page 8 over the two lines in the centre of the map. Now use the tracing to answer the following questions.
- What is north-east of A?
- What is south-west of A?
- What is north of A?
- What is west of A?

● Fill in the gaps with the correct direction.
- The bank is _____ of the aircraft.
- The windmill is _____ of the bank.
- The ship is _____ of the hospital.
- The library is _____ of the bank.

● Which directions would you go if you went:
- from the hospital to the bank?
- from the telephone box to the mosque?
- from the mosque to the library?
- from the aircraft to the telephone box?

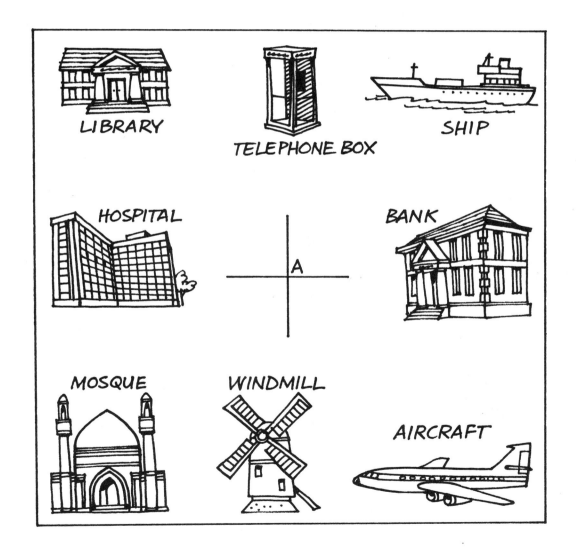

● ESSENTIALS FOR GEOGRAPHY: Distance and direction

● Name _____

Signpost map

● Look at Joanne's signpost map of the people in her classroom.
- Who is north of Joanne? _____
- Who is south of Joanne? _____
- Who is south-east of Joanne? _____
- Who is north-west of Joanne? _____
- Who is west of Joanne? _____
- Who is east of Joanne? _____
- Who is north-east of Joanne? _____
- Who is south-west of Joanne? _____

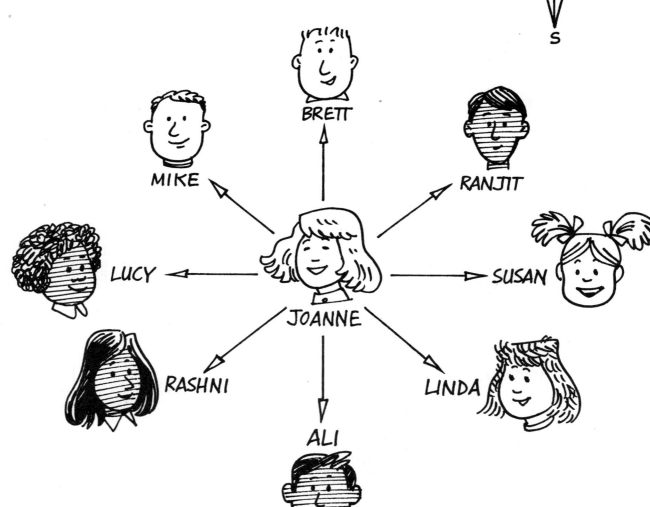

● ESSENTIALS FOR GEOGRAPHY: Distance and direction

● Name _____

Signpost map at the show

Lucy has gone to a show. The signpost map tells her where the different events can be found.

● Look at signpost map and answer the questions.
- Which way would Lucy go to the vegetable contest? _____
- Which way would Lucy go to the ice cream stall? _____
- Which way would Lucy go to see the sheepdogtrials? _____
- Which way would Lucy go to see the wrestling? _____
- If Lucy goes west what will she see? _____
- If Lucy goes east what will she see? _____
- Which way will Lucy need to turn to see the cake stalls? _____
- Which way will Lucy need to turn to see the horse jumping? _____

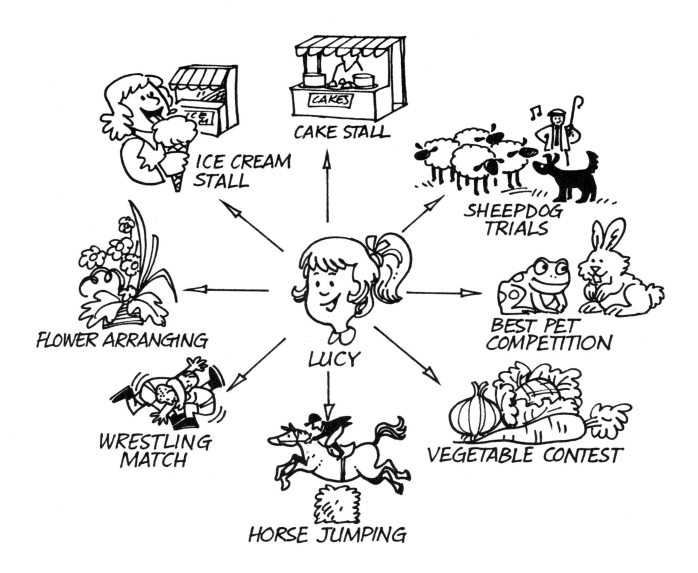

ESSENTIALS FOR GEOGRAPHY: Distance and direction

- Name _____

Signpost map of Linton

- Look at the map of Linton below. Imagine you are standing at point 1, facing in the direction shown by the arrow. Complete the signpost map in box A by writing down what you can see in each direction. The first one has been done for you.

- Now in box B fill in the signpost map as if you are standing at point 2 facing in the direction of the arrow.

- In boxes C, D, E and F fill in the signpost maps for points 3, 4, 5 and 6.

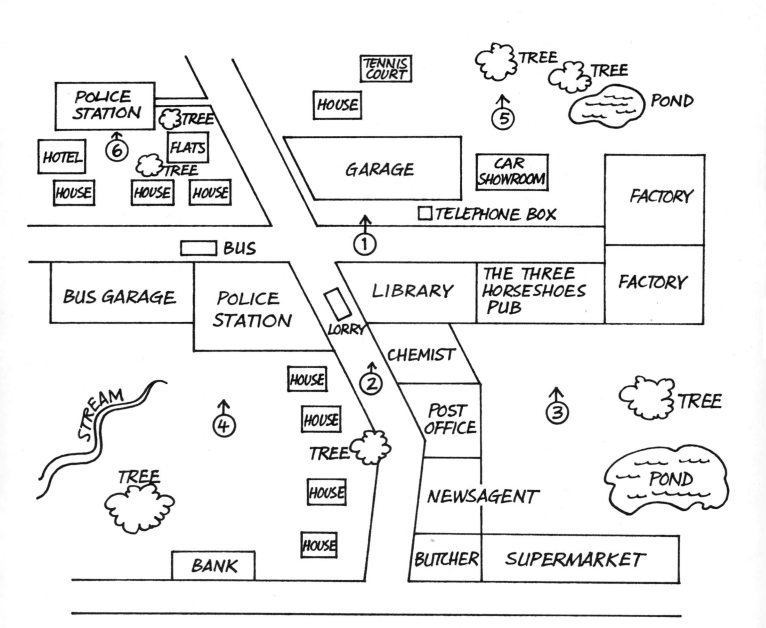

ESSENTIALS FOR GEOGRAPHY: Distance and direction

Signpost map of Linton (continued)

Point 1 — Box A	Point 2 — Box B
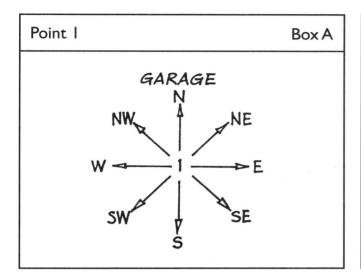	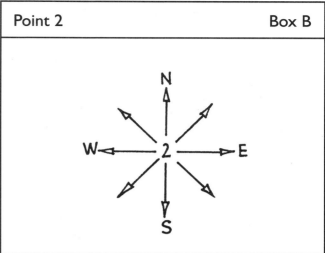

Point 3 — Box C	Point 4 — Box D
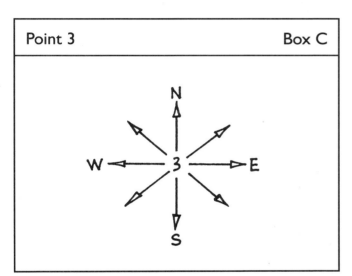	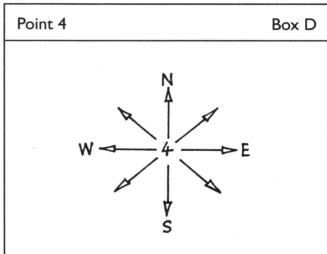

Point 6 — Box E	Point 5 — Box F
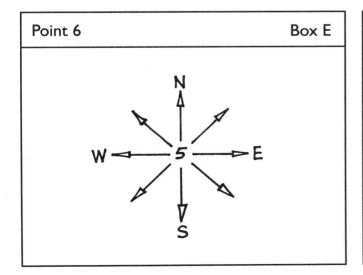	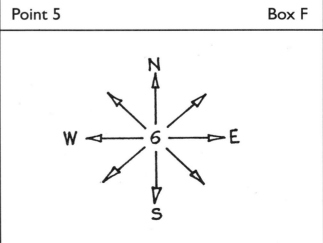

ESSENTIALS FOR GEOGRAPHY: Distance and direction

● Name _____

Directions from Britain

● Use an atlas together with the compass to make a list of the countries that are to be found in different directions from Britain.

North
1. _____

North-west
1. _____
2. _____

North-east
1. _____
2. _____
3. _____

West
1. _____
2. _____

East
1. _____
2. _____
3. _____
4. _____

South-west
1. _____
2. _____

South-east
1. _____
2. _____
3. _____
4. _____

South
1. _____
2. _____
3. _____
4. _____

● ESSENTIALS FOR GEOGRAPHY: Distance and direction

● Name _____

Directions in Europe

● Look at the map of Europe then answer the questions below:
- Which country is north of Germany? _____
- Which country is south-west of France? _____
- In which direction is Portugal from Spain? _____
- Which country is north of Italy? _____
- In which direction is Norway from Denmark? _____
- If you travelled from Sweden to Germany in which direction would you be travelling? _____
- A wind blowing from Belgium to Italy would be coming from which direction? _____
- Which country is south-east of Italy? _____

ESSENTIALS FOR GEOGRAPHY: Distance and direction

- Name _____

Directions in the USA

- Look at the map opposite then answer the following questions:
- Which state is north-west of Colorado? _____
- Which state is south of Kansas? _____
- Which state is north-east of Iowa? _____
- Which state is west of Tennessee? _____
- Which state is east of Alabama? _____

- Name three States south-east of Washington.
1. _____
2. _____
3. _____

- Name three States north-west of Utah.
1. _____
2. _____
3. _____

- Name three States west of Georgia.
1. _____
2. _____
3. _____

- Name five States south of Ohio.
1. _____
2. _____
3. _____
4. _____
5. _____

- Name four States north-east of Alabama.
1. _____
2. _____
3. _____
4. _____

- Draw in red a route through all the US States shown on the map opposite from New York to California, naming each state passed in a straight line from east to west.

Directions in the USA (continued)

Name _____

ESSENTIALS FOR GEOGRAPHY: Distance and direction

19

• Name _____

Wood island

• Use your ruler to measure the distances on Wood island in centimetres. Measure along the straight lines.

- The distance from North City to Falcon Cragg is _____ cm.
- The distance from Ridgeton to North City is _____ cm.
- The distance from North Point to Eastville is _____ cm.
- The distance from Motown to Ridgeton is _____ cm.
- The distance from Motown to Shark Cove is _____ cm.
- The distance from Westport to Motown is _____ cm.
- Which place is nearest to Westport? _____
- If you travel from Westport to Falcon Cragg which towns must you pass? _____
- Travelling from Westport to Motown, which town is on your left? _____

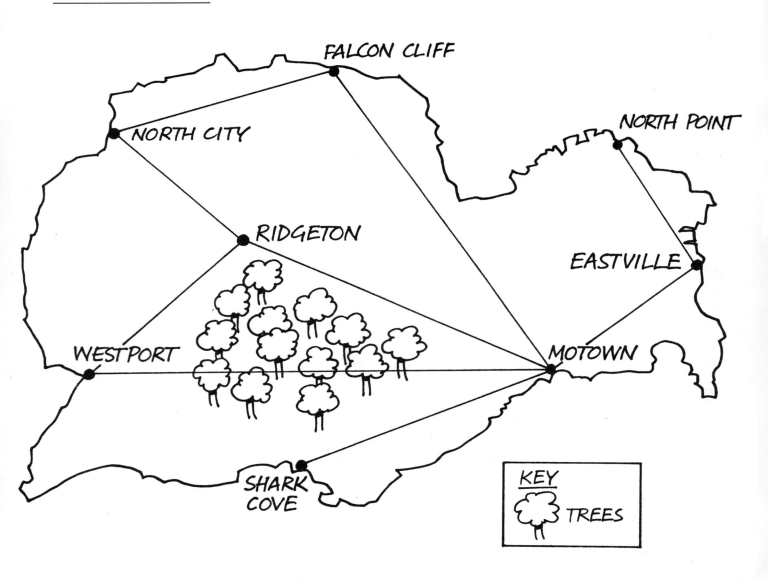

ESSENTIALS FOR GEOGRAPHY: Distance and direction

● Name _____

Distances near school

On the map below, 1 centimetre represents 10 metres on the ground. From Mike's house to Ann's house it is 2 cm on the map. This represents 20 metres on the ground.

● Measure these distances:
- from the newsagent to the park _____ cm. which represents _____ m.
- from the park to the leisure centre _____ cm. which represents _____ m.
- from the garage to the bank _____ cm. which represents _____ m.
- from Ann's house to the park _____ cm. which represents _____ m.
- from Ann's house to the leisure centre _____ cm. which represents _____ m.
- from John's house to Show Lane _____ cm. which represents _____ m.
- from Mike's house to the school _____ cm. which represents _____ m.

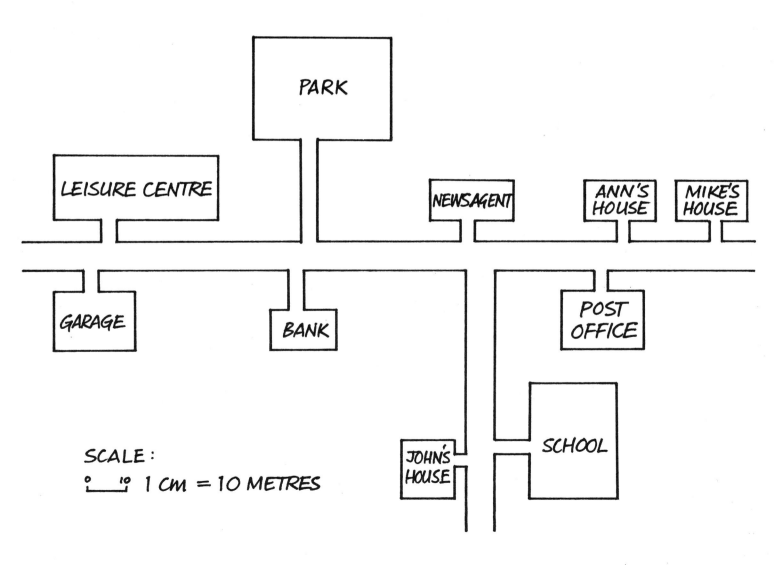

SCALE: 1 CM = 10 METRES

ESSENTIALS FOR GEOGRAPHY: Distance and direction

● Name _____

Flying from Birmingham

The map below shows some of the main cities of the British Isles. The scale of the map is 1cm = 50km.
● Draw straight lines from Birmingham to each of the towns shown.
● Measure the length of each line and work out how many kilometres it is from Birmingham to each one, for example, Birmingham to London 3 cm = 150 km.

● ESSENTIALS FOR GEOGRAPHY: Distance and direction

● Name _____

Flying from Zurich

The map below shows some of the main cities in Europe.
● Draw a straight line from Zurich to each of the other cities marked on the map.
● Use the scale (1cm = 150km) to work out the distance in kilometres between Zurich and each city.

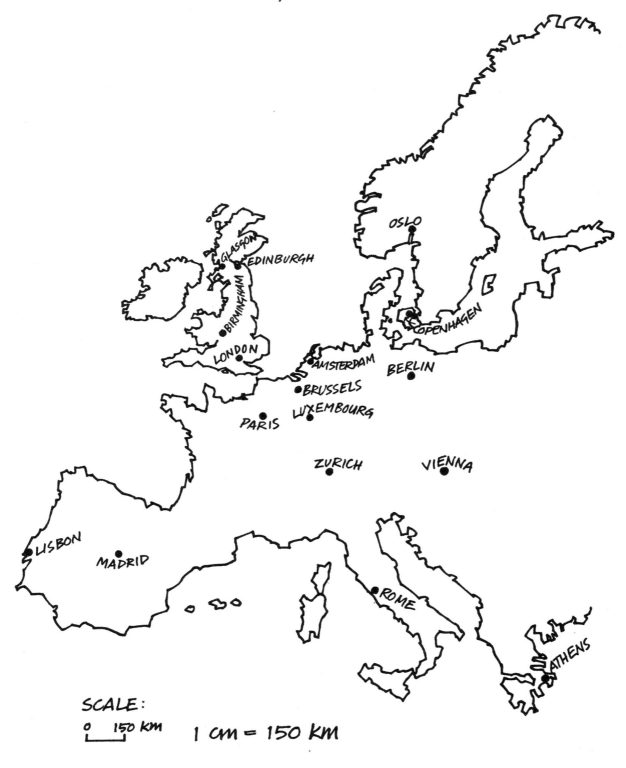

SCALE:
0 150 km   1 cm = 150 km

● ESSENTIALS FOR GEOGRAPHY: Distance and direction

● Name _____

Distances in the western USA

● Use the scale and a ruler to work out the straight line distance between these US cities:
- Denver to Salt Lake City _____
- San Francisco to Reno _____
- Alberquerque to Denver _____
- Las Vegas to Phoenix _____
- Seattle to Spokane _____
- Helena to Bismark _____

● How far would you travel on each of these air tours:
- Los Angeles, Las Vegas, Phoenix, Alberquerque, Denver, Salt Lake City, Reno, San Francisco, Los Angeles _____
- Seattle, Portland, Boise, Salt Lake City, Denver, Rapid City, Bismark, Helena, Spokane and Seattle _____

SCALE:
0 260 520 KM   1 CM = 260 KM

● ESSENTIALS FOR GEOGRAPHY: Distance and direction

● Name _____

Distances in the eastern USA

● Use the scale and a ruler to work out the straight line distance between New York and each other city on the map.

● Answer the following questions:

- Which city is nearest to New York? _____
- Which city is furthest from New York? _____
- How far would you travel if you went on this air tour: _____

From New York to Washington, Charleston, Miami, New Orleans, Dallas, Atlanta, Duluth and back to New York.

SCALE:
0 260 520 km   1 cm = 260 km

ESSENTIALS FOR GEOGRAPHY: Distance and direction

- Name _____

Distances around

● Using a sheet of tracing paper, copy the circles shown below and add on the metre distances, together with the cross in the centre of the diagram.

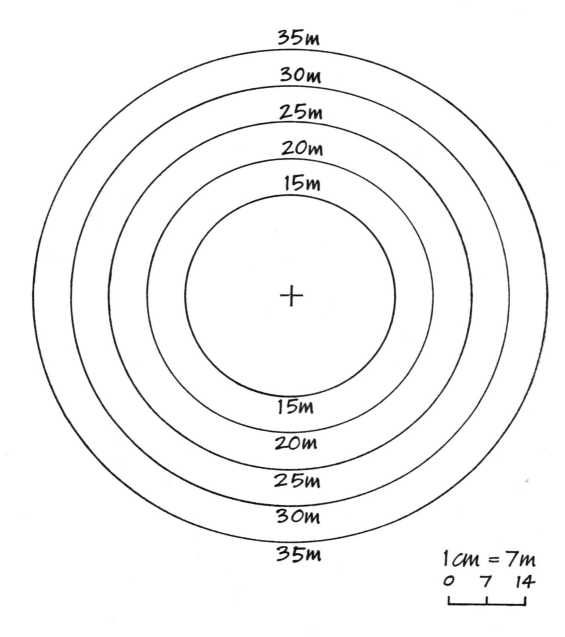

● Put the cross on the tracing over the cross on the school on the map on page 27. Make sure the tracing is upright.
● Write out the sentences below filling in the correct distances from your tracing. The first one has been done for you:
- The bus stop lies within a radius of 35 metres of the school.
- The post box lies within a radius of _____ metres of the school.
- The telephone box lies within a radius of _____ metres of the school.

● Name _____

Distances around (continued)

- The pond lies within a radius of _____ metres of the school.
- The tree lies within a radius of _____ metres of the school.
- The washing line lies within a radius of _____ metres of the school.
● Use the scale to calculate the length of:

   a) the supermarket _____ m   d) bank _____ m

   b) the car park _____ m   e) building society _____ m

   c) the travel agent shop _____ m f) video rental _____ m

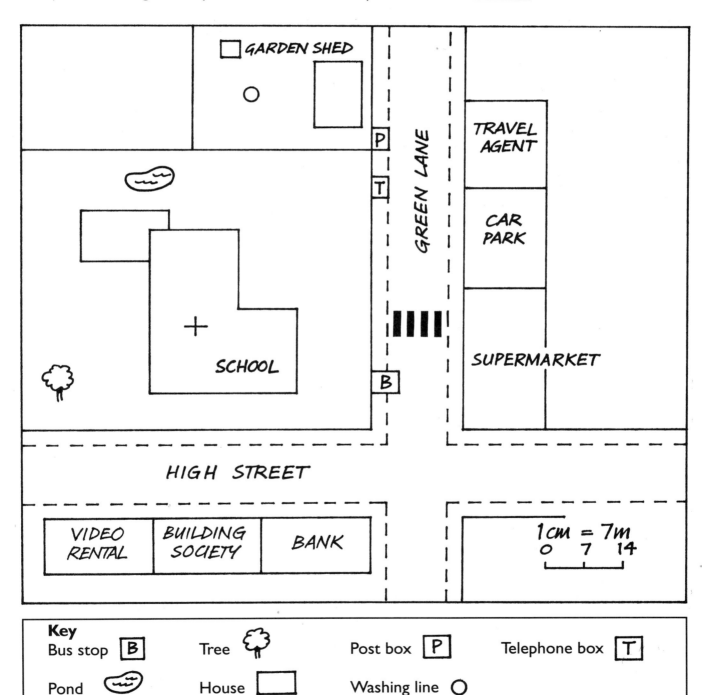

ESSENTIALS FOR GEOGRAPHY: Distance and direction

● Name _____

Direct distance, actual distance

The **direct distance** is the straight-line distance between places.
The **actual distance** is the distance along a route between two places. The route between the places usually has to bend around corners and curves so is often longer than the straight-line distance.

● Use a ruler to measure the **straight-line** distance and a piece of string or wool to measure the **actual distance** along roads, between each of these places:

	Straight-line distance	Actual distance
from Sue's house to school	300 metres	1800 metres
from Sharon's house to the telephone box		
from Keith's house to Sue's house		
from the church to the post office		
from John's house to Sue's house		
from Sharon's house to John's house		
from Keith's house to John's house		
from Sue's house to the post office		

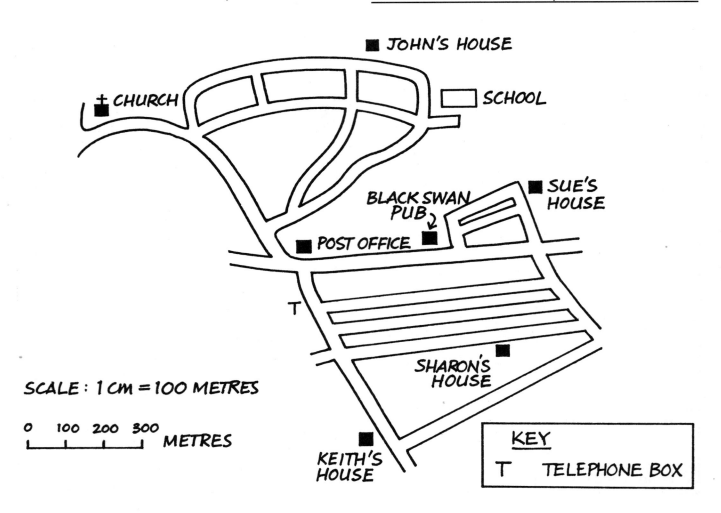

SCALE: 1 CM = 100 METRES

0 100 200 300 METRES

KEY
T   TELEPHONE BOX

● ESSENTIALS FOR GEOGRAPHY: Distance and direction

- Name _____

More direct distances, actual distances

● Use a ruler to measure **direct distance** and a piece of string or wool to measure **actual distance** along roads between each of these places:

	Direct line distance	Actual distance
from Luke's house to the newsagent		
from Lucy's house to the leisure centre		
from Ali's house to the hairdresser's shop		
from Luke's house to Ali's house		
from Rashni's house to Lucy's house		
from Rashni's house to DIY store		
from Lucy's house to the factory		
from Luke's house to Lucy's house		
from Rashni's house to Luke's house		

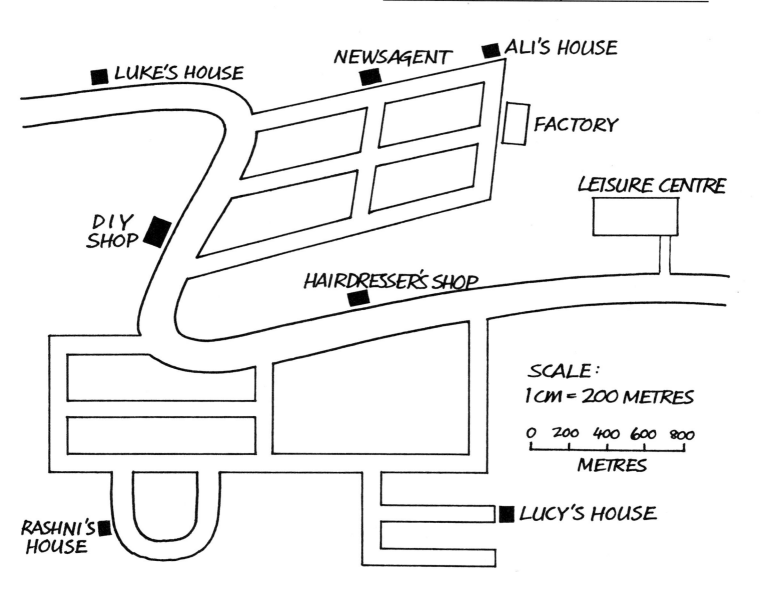

SCALE: 1CM = 200 METRES

ESSENTIALS FOR GEOGRAPHY: Distance and direction

Whitby – air view and map

The map and the drawing on this and the next page show the central part of the seaside town of Whitby in North Yorkshire. The drawing shows the oblique air view of Whitby.

- Using the scale, what is the actual distance of:
- the Abbey from the church? _____
- the Abbey from the bandstand? _____
- the Abbey from the railway station? _____
- the church from the hospital? _____

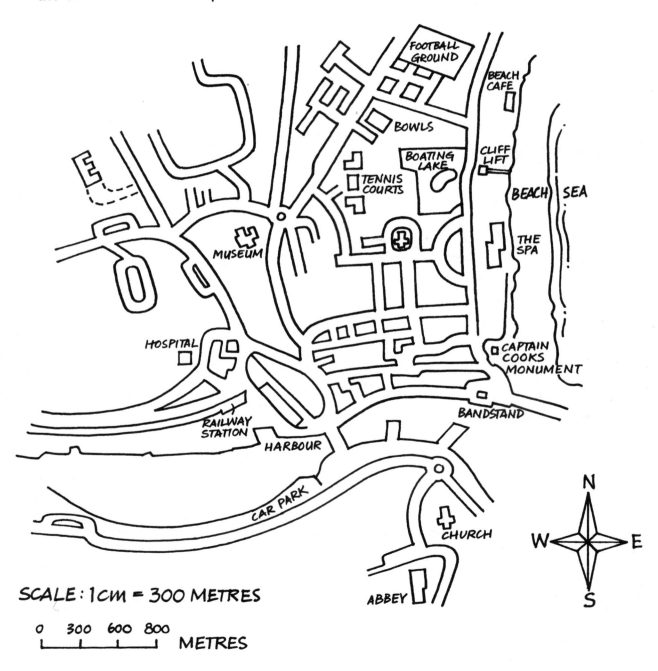

SCALE: 1cm = 300 METRES

ESSENTIALS FOR GEOGRAPHY: Distance and direction

● Name _____

Whitby – air view and map (continued)

● Use the information given on the map to label each of the following features on the drawing:
- the Abbey
- the church
- the river
- the beach
- the sea
- the bridge
- the harbour
- the bandstand
- the Spa
- the boating lake

● In which direction was the artist facing when he drew the picture?

ESSENTIALS FOR GEOGRAPHY: Distance and direction

Planning a classroom

The map below is a plan of a classroom. On this map 2 cms is equal to 1 metre on the ground.

- Using the shapes and sizes shown on the map, measure and cut out this furniture:
  - 10 small tables
  - 4 large tables
  - 3 storage units
  - 30 chairs

- Now arrange the furniture in the classroom.

- Colour in the furniture and add it to the key.

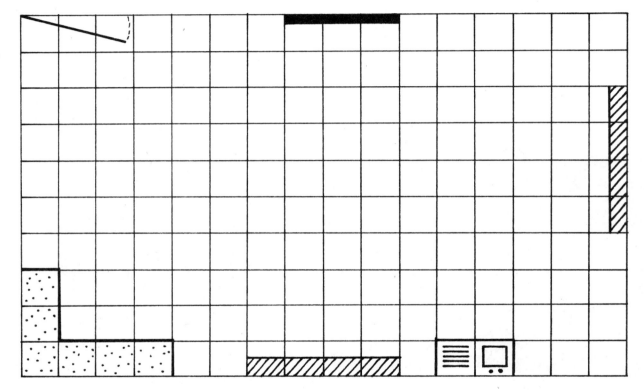

SCALE:
2 CMS = 1 METRE

0 0.5 1 2 METRES

TABLES 0.5M × 1M
STORAGE UNITS 0.5M × 1M
TABLES 1M × 1M
CHAIRS 0.25M × 0.25M

KEY
- DOOR
- SINK
- CUPBOARD
- SHELVES
- CHALK BOARD

ESSENTIALS FOR GEOGRAPHY: Distance and direction